Living on Other Worlds

By Gregory Vogt

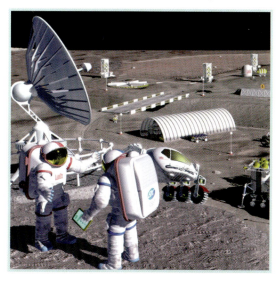

OUR UNIVERSE

www.raintreepublishers.co.uk
Visit our website to find out more information about Raintree books.

To order:
 Phone 44 (0) 1865 888112
Send a fax to 44 (0) 1865 314091
 Visit the Raintree Bookshop at www.raintreepublishers.co.uk to browse our catalogue and order online.

First published in Great Britain by Raintree Publishers, Halley Court, Jordan Hill, Oxford OX2 8EJ, part of Harcourt Education.
Raintree is a registered trademark of Harcourt Education Ltd.

Design: Jo Hinton-Malivoire and Tinstar Design (www.tinstar.co.uk), Jo Sapwell (www.tipani.co.uk)
Illustrations: Art Construction
Picture Research: Maria Joannou and Su Alexander
Production: Jonathan Smith

Originated by Dot Gradations Ltd
Printed and bound in Hong Kong and China by South China Printing

ISBN 1 844 21420 6
07 06 05 04 03
10 9 8 7 6 5 4 3 2 1

British Library Cataloguing in Publication Data
Vogt, Gregory
1.Life on other planets –
Exploration – Juvenile literature
I.Title
576.8'39

A full catalogue record for this book is available from the British Library.

Acknowledgements
The publishers would like to thank the following for permission to reproduce photographs:
Cover Photo:
Digital Stock, 9, 10; NASA, all remaining interior photographs.

Content consultant
David Jewitt
Professor of Astronomy
University of Hawaii Institute for Astronomy.

Contents

Any words appearing in the text in bold, **like this**, are explained in the glossary.

Diagram of a Moon home

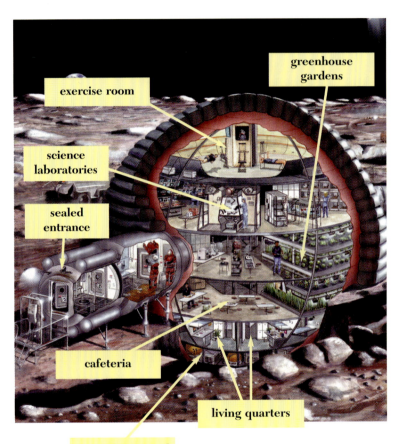

greenhouse gardens

exercise room

science laboratories

sealed entrance

cafeteria

living quarters

power source and storage area

A quick look at other planets

What other planets could people live on?
Scientists are studying ways to send people to live on the
Moon and on Mars. Some people think Jupiter's moon
Europa might also be a good place to set up a colony.

Why might people want to live on other planets?
One day, the Earth may become crowded with too
many people. People might want to live on other
planets where it is less crowded. People might want
to use the natural **resources** of other planets. They
might also enjoy the excitement of exploring and
living in new places.

How might people travel to other planets?
People would probably travel in spacecraft that are
pushed into space by powerful rockets.

How might people survive on other planets?
People might have to bring air, food, water, building
materials and other things with them to set up new
homes on other planets.

Sun

Mercury

Venus

Earth

This diagram shows the location of planets in our solar system. The sizes and distances are not to scale.

Mars

Jupiter

Saturn

Uranus

Neptune

Pluto

No place like home

People live on the surface of the planet Earth. The Earth is one of the nine planets that travel around the Sun in paths called **orbits**. Planets orbit the Sun in a certain order. The closest planet to the Sun is Mercury. Venus, the Earth and Mars are next. These planets are often called the inner planets. The outer planets orbit further away from the Sun. These planets are called Jupiter, Saturn, Uranus, Neptune and Pluto.

The Earth is the only planet scientists know of that has living things, but one day people may want to live on other planets in space. First they need to find good planets to move to. Mercury or Venus would not be good choices. Mercury does not have any air for us to breathe and the air on Venus is poisonous. Both of these planets are also too hot to support life.

Living on the Earth

Living things on the Earth would die without the Sun. People, plants and animals need the Sun's light and heat to live. The Earth is at the perfect distance from the Sun for living things.

People use the Earth's **resources**. Over time, people have learned how to use the Earth's resources to make things, such as buildings, cars, ships and aeroplanes.

People live on nearly every part of the Earth. Not every part of the Earth is healthy for humans. Some parts are too cold, while others are too hot. But people have found ways to live in these places. In very cold places, people wear warm clothes and live in warm houses. In hot places, people wear light clothes. Some people live in air-conditioned homes.

Other planets and moons do not have the same natural resources as the Earth. In the future, people's skills for building things will make moving to these other places possible. Some people may want to move to Mars or the Moon. These planets do not have the same air, water or soil as the Earth. But many scientists believe they can build things to make it possible to live in these places.

The Earth has many natural resources, such as forests and water.

> We need water to drink and animals or plants to eat.

What we need to live

We need many things to live. We need water to drink. The Earth is nicknamed the blue planet because of its water. Unlike other planets, the Earth's surface is mostly liquid water. Seas, lakes and rivers cover about 70 per cent of the Earth's surface.

The Earth provides us with the food that we need to live. Lots of people eat fish and other animals.

Large land masses called continents cover roughly 30 per cent of the Earth. We use the soil on the continents to grow vegetables, fruits and cereals to eat.

We need air to breathe. The Earth's air, or **atmosphere**, is a layer of gases that surrounds the planet. It is made mostly of nitrogen and oxygen. People need to breathe oxygen to live.

The atmosphere also protects the planet. It blocks rays from the Sun, like X-rays and gamma rays, that are harmful to humans.

The Earth's air also moves the Sun's heat around the world. This helps control temperatures on the Earth's surface. The weight of the atmosphere (atmospheric pressure) is also important. It stops liquids boiling away. Without atmospheric pressure the seas, and even your blood, would boil.

People also need **gravity**. Gravity is a force that attracts all objects to each other. The Earth's gravity stops people from floating away into space. Gravity pulls on a person's body every time he or she moves. Gravity's pull keeps the body's muscles working.

Today, there are many satellites circling the Earth. A satellite took this picture of the Earth from space.

Wild ideas

Many people have dreamed of travelling into space. Some have wondered what it would be like to live on other planets. There are many books and films about what it would be like to live on other planets.

About 140 years ago, a man called Edward Everett Hale wrote a story about a **satellite**. A satellite is a small object that orbits around a bigger object in space.

In the story, a group of people built a brick moon 60 metres wide. They planned to use huge, spinning wheels to toss the moon into space. They hoped that sailors could use the brick moon to find their way across the oceans.

By accident, they launched the ball before it was ready. Workers and their families were on the ball when it was tossed into space. The people lived and grew food on the brick moon. Family and friends on the Earth tossed books and other things up to them. The things that missed orbited the brick moon.

Today, the brick moon story seems silly. But it was the first story to think of the idea of a space station amd imagine what it would be like to live on one.

Astronauts can look down at the Earth from space stations.

Space stations

A space station is an artificial **satellite** in space where people can live. Astronauts inside space stations get to do things other people only dream about. They can look at the Earth below. They see its mountains, forests, deserts, cities, ice and clouds. They can look at the sky overhead, filled with countless stars that look much brighter than the stars seen from the Earth.

Solar panels are attached to the outside of space stations. The panels collect energy from the Sun. They turn the Sun's energy into electricity for the space station.

Astronauts inside space stations do experiments. They study animals and plants. They think of better ways for humans to live and work in space. They also study the Earth.

This is what the inside of a space station module looks like.

Living in a space station

Space stations are made of tubular rooms called **modules**. Each module serves a different purpose. Large space stations have several modules. Small space stations may have only one or two modules.

Because there is so little **gravity** in space, astronauts float inside space stations. They need special equipment to help them live and work.

Astronauts live in the habitation module. They eat the same foods they do on the Earth, but their food may float away, so they keep it in tubes or plastic-covered containers. They use scissors to open the food containers.

The module has a special toilet. The toilet uses air to pull floating waste into a container. Some space stations have a sealed unit that serves as a shower. If the unit were not sealed, water would float around the module. Astronauts dry off with a vacuum hose. In space stations that have no showers, astronauts take sponge baths.

Astronauts sleep in sleeping bags that are attached to the station. This prevents them from floating around while they sleep. Astronauts place small fans near their heads. The fans blow away the **carbon dioxide** gas they breathe out while they sleep. If they did not have fans, they would breathe in carbon dioxide instead of oxygen.

Some space stations have exercise machines. Astronauts lose muscle and bone density if they live without gravity for too long. Exercising helps stop muscle loss and bone damage.

Astronauts work in science modules. There may be more than one science module. This is where scientists perform experiments, such as growing food.

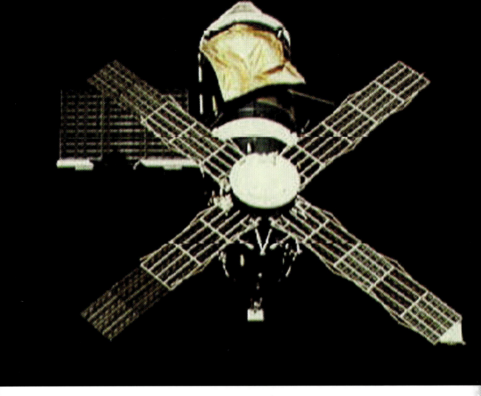

Early space stations

The **Soviet Union** launched the first space station in 1971. They called it *Salyut 1*. The space station was a long tube with wing-like solar panels. A crew of three cosmonauts flew to the station. *Cosmonaut* is the Russian word for astronaut. The cosmonauts lived in *Salyut 1* for three weeks.

The USA's National Aeronautics and Space Administration (NASA) built the space station *Skylab*.

Skylab entered the Earth's **orbit** in 1973. Also tube-shaped, it was larger than *Salyut 1*. Three different teams of astronauts lived on *Skylab*. One team stayed on board for 84 days. Each team performed science experiments. In 1979, *Skylab* burned up in the Earth's atmosphere.

Mir

The Soviet Union launched the first part of the *Mir* Space Station in 1986. The main module was one long tube. Later, they launched more modules. Cosmonauts connected the modules. Each new module made *Mir* larger.

Every part of *Mir* had its own purpose. There was a small spacecraft at the front of Mir. If there were problems inside the station, cosmonauts could use the spacecraft to escape. Behind the escape spacecraft were docking ports. Other spacecraft could attach to the ports. Docking spacecraft brought new supplies and cosmonauts to the station. Cosmonauts used other parts of *Mir* to perform experiments, eat, exercise and sleep. *Mir* even had a library.

Mir remained in orbit for 15 years. In March 2001, *Mir* re-entered the Earth's atmosphere above Nadi, in Fiji, and crashed into the Pacific Ocean.

International Space Station

The International Space Station is the newest space station. People in sixteen countries around the world are working together to build it.

The station is being built in stages over several years. Parts of the station are in space now. Spacecraft will continue to bring new pieces and modules to the station. Astronauts will connect the pieces. It will take them at least 1,500 hours to put the station together. Scientists hope to finish the station in 2005 or 2006.

The International Space Station will be 73 metres wide and will weigh about 450 metric tons. Lots of modules will be connected to each other. Astronauts will live and work inside the modules. Large solar panels will make electricity for the station.

The robot arms attached to the outside of the station will move equipment around. Space shuttles will come from the Earth with supplies. The robot arms will help unload these supplies.

Life on the International Space Station

Up to seven astronauts will stay on the space station for between three and six months at a time. The station will become their home.

Astronauts will sleep in sleeping bags that are attached to the wall of a small room the size of a telephone booth. Inside the room there will be a reading light. There may also be a computer for sending e-mail messages to families back on Earth.

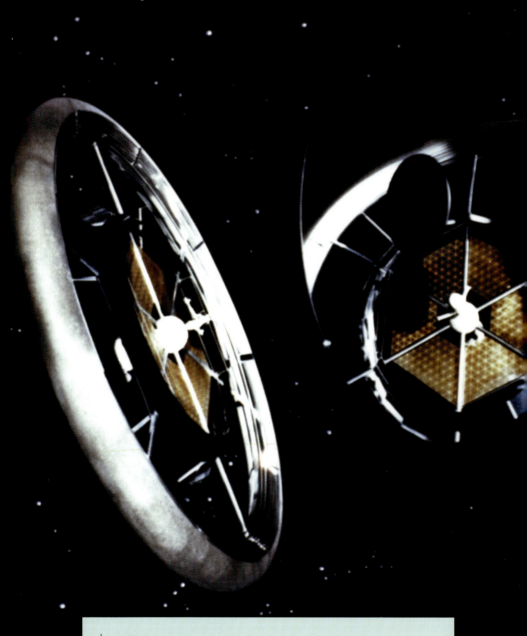

This is an artist's drawing of what a space city might look like.

Space cities

In the future, people may decide to live in space. Space stations will not be big enough. People will have to build space cities where thousands of people can live.

Space cities will probably be the shape of giant wheels that spin. The spin will produce a force equal to that of gravity. The force will pull on people's bodies and keep their muscles healthy. It will also mean that people can walk normally around the city.

Energy from the Sun will be important to space cities. Huge solar panels will use sunlight to make electricity. People will use sunlight to grow plants inside large greenhouses.

The design of the city may be a lot like cities on the Earth. There may be blocks of flats where people can live. Between the flats there might be small parks with trees, grass and ponds.

Many people think space cities could be built with materials **mined** on the Moon. Other materials could be brought from the Earth by rockets. People in space cities could trade products they make for supplies they need from the Earth.

The Moon is covered with craters and grey, dust-like soil.

Moving to the Moon

The Moon is a rocky ball 384,400 kilometres (238,900 miles) from the Earth. It is 3475 kilometres (2160 miles) in diameter. Some people think that in the future, humans will live on the Moon.

The Moon's surface is different from the Earth's. The Moon has no liquid water on its surface. Instead, there are light grey and black rocks and dust-like soil. Some tall mountains and cliffs rise from the ground.

Large craters cover the Moon's surface. A crater is a large, bowl-shaped hole in the ground. Sometimes space rocks called **meteorites** crash into the Moon. They cause explosions that leave more craters on the surface of the Moon. Crater's can be 2200 kilometres (1400 miles) across. The Moon's smallest craters can barely hold a grain of sand.

 This *Apollo* astronaut is exploring the Moon.

Moon exploration

The US *Apollo* space programme began in the 1960s. Some *Apollo* spacecraft **orbited** the Moon and gathered information. Others landed on the Moon.

   Each *Apollo* spacecraft had two **modules**. The first one was a command module. It was a cone-like capsule. The astronauts lived in the command module during the mission. It was built to orbit the Moon and then return to the Earth. The lunar module was the second module. Scientists designed it to land on the Moon.

Apollo astronauts first landed on the Moon in 1969 during the *Apollo 11* mission. In 1972, the *Apollo 17* mission landed on the Moon. The Apollo 17 astronauts were the last astronauts to land on the Moon.

In total, twelve astronauts have so far walked on the Moon. On every landing, two astronauts climbed out of their spacecraft and explored the Moon. They did experiments and collected rocks to bring home.

Scientists learned many things from studying Moon rocks. They discovered that Moon rocks are made of many elements, such as iron and titanium. People could use the materials in these rocks to build space cities on the Moon.

Some scientists are studying ways to set up a colony on the Moon. The first colony will probably be used as a **mining** operation. Workers would mine valuable materials found on the Moon. People would bring the materials back to the Earth to use in buildings and other projects.

> ▲ This is an artist's drawing of what a reusable Moon rocket might look like.

Conditions on the Moon

Moon-dwellers would need a lot of special equipment. Difficult conditions exist on the Moon. For example, it has no **atmosphere**. People will need air to breathe inside space cities or spacesuits while they are on the Moon. They will need a way to recycle the air so that it stays fresh. People will also need a way to keep the air from escaping into space.

Temperatures on the Moon vary widely. In the sunlight, the temperature on the Moon rises to about 107 °C. Out of the Sun, it can drop to –156 °C. People cannot easily live with such extreme changes in temperature. They will need machines to keep the temperature in the space cities or in their spacesuits at the right level.

Getting there

The Moon is far away. Powerful rockets will be needed to take spacecraft so far into space.

Rockets use a lot of fuel to go to space. The *Apollo* spacecraft used the *Saturn V* rocket to go to the Moon. The rocket was 111 metres tall and weighed 2700 metric tons. More than half the rocket's weight was fuel to push the rocket upwards. *Saturn V* rockets could only be used once.

Going to the Moon to live will require rockets that can be used over and over again. One rocket could take people from the Earth. They could meet another rocket in the Earth's **orbit**. People could change rockets and travel on the second rocket to the Moon. The first rocket could then return to the Earth to pick up more fuel and more passengers.

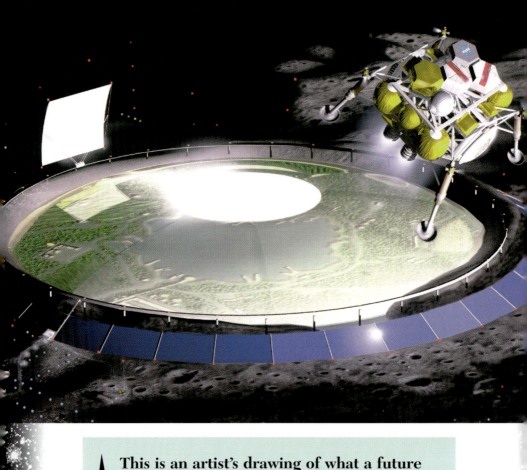

This is an artist's drawing of what a future city on the Moon might look like.

Costly trip

Travelling into space is very expensive. Today, it costs about £14,500 for each kilogram of material carried to space. Future Moon rockets will be cheaper, but still very expensive. People will not be able to pack much to bring with them.

Instead of bringing items from the Earth, people will find things they need on the Moon. Moon rocks contain metals and materials to make glass. There may be ice in deep craters on the Moon. People can use different processes to turn melted ice into water, oxygen and rocket fuel. People could use solar panels to collect sunlight for heat and electricity.

Underground cities

Colonizing the Moon may be difficult. The first Moon colonists might have to live in the spacecraft that brought them there. The spacecraft could have four legs. A small cabin, containing air, water, food, beds, tables, tools and a toilet, might sit on top of the legs. Colonists could look outside at the Moon's surface through windows in the sides of the cabin.

The cabin might have two door-like hatches to go outside. Colonists could open one hatch and step inside a small room, called an air-lock. After they close the hatch, the air inside the room would be sucked back into the cabin. Then they would open the outer hatch and climb down a ladder.

Other colonists might come to live on the Moon. They might bring inflatable (blow-up) houses. People might use inflatable tunnels to connect the houses. Then they could cover the houses with moon soil to protect them. Eventually, they could create huge underground cities.

▲ **This is a drawing of what a mining machine might look like. It is processing Moon rocks.**

Life on the Moon

At first, food for people on the Moon might have to come from the Earth. Later, people might grow their own food. Colonists might use greenhouses to grow their food. Moon greenhouses could have many long trays. Colonists could fill the trays with Moon soil and fertilizer from the Earth and plant wheat and soya beans close together. They could also grow other plants, such as lettuce, tomatoes and sweet potatoes.

The greenhouse could have an Earth-like **atmosphere** and a watering system. The plants should be watered every day, so they do not become too dry.

Colonists would need to find ways to give the plants enough light. Every night and every day on the Moon is fourteen Earth days long. Batteries could store electricity for the long nights. Electricity could power lights in the greenhouses. The lights could take the place of sunlight and keep plants healthy.

Moon farmers would have to watch their crops carefully. During the Moon day, sunlight could make the greenhouses too hot. Colonists would need air conditioning to stop the plants being cooked.

Many of the people living on the Moon could be scientists. They could explore the Moon and look for rocks and minerals. Some could use telescopes to study objects in deep space. Other people could build new buildings and grow food.

The Moon city could be a popular place for people on the Earth to visit. Tourists could enjoy the effects of a smaller gravitational force. For example, they could jump six times higher on the Moon than they could on the Earth.

The surface of Mars is mostly dry.

Moving to Mars

Some scientists believe the planet Mars may be one of the best choices for a future human colony. Mars is the fourth planet from the Sun and **orbits** the Sun at a distance of 228 million kilometres (142 million miles). It takes Mars 687 Earth days to go around the Sun once.

The Earth and Mars are very different. Mars is a smaller planet than the Earth. Mars has seasons like the Earth, but they are about twice as long. The surface of Mars is very dry. It has little or no flowing water. Red dust and rocks cover the ground. A huge canyon stretches one-fifth of the way around the planet. Huge volcanoes rise up from the planet's surface.

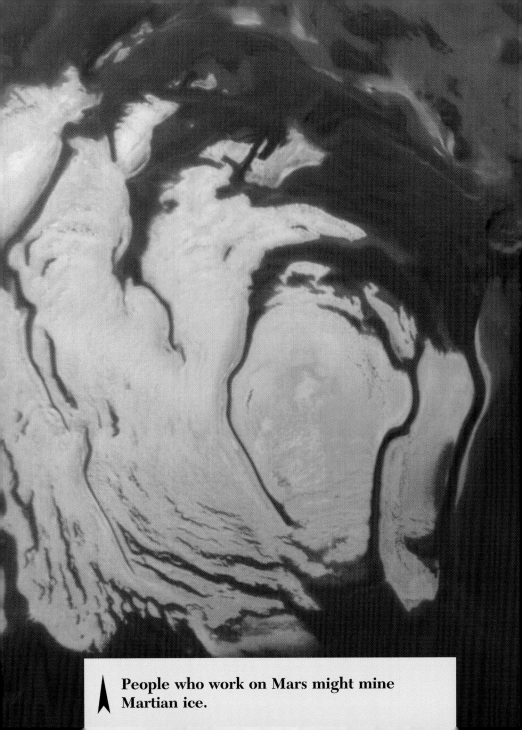

People who work on Mars might mine Martian ice.

Difficult conditions

People who move to Mars will have to prepare for difficult conditions. Mars does not have very much air. Most of the air is **carbon dioxide** gas. People need oxygen to breathe. They would die if there was only carbon dioxide to breathe.

Most of the surface of Mars is as dry as a desert. Mars colonists would have to bring or find water to drink. Scientists think that, in some places, water is frozen beneath the surface. Colonists may be able to **mine** the ice. They could melt it for water. Scientists think that new pictures of Mars show that, at times, water has flooded the surface from beneath the surface. Colonists may be able to find and use these liquid water sources.

Mars often has bad weather. Strong winds stir up the dust and huge dust storms occasionally blanket the whole planet. The storms can last for months at a time. The temperatures on Mars change a great deal from day to night. They are hotter during the day and colder at night. The temperature on warm days can be up to 21 °C, but it can drop to −126 °C on cold nights.

Getting there

Astronauts must travel millions of kilometres to reach Mars. Most trips would take place when Mars is closest to the Earth, once every 26 months. The trip would be very long and dangerous. It would take people at least four months to reach Mars from the Earth. They would need to use large, powerful rockets. Carrying enough food, water and air for the trip could be a problem.

Scientists are trying to find faster ways to get to Mars. If the trip were shorter, astronauts would need fewer supplies, but scientists would have to invent a faster rocket for this to happen.

Scientists are trying several new rocket designs. Some new rockets are designed to use different kinds of fuel. In these rockets, electricity and magnets shoot out tiny particles. Energy from the particles powers the rockets. These are much faster than other rockets, but scientists need to do much more testing before these rockets are ready to use.

Scientists are also inventing a new kind of spacecraft. These new spacecraft will be a combination of rocket-type spacecraft and aeroplanes.

▲ **This rocket is taking a Mars space probe into space.**

Scientists never aim rockets directly at Mars. The planet is always moving through space as it orbits the Sun. Mars would be in another place by the time the rockets arrived. Scientists use computers to work out how long the trip to Mars will take. If the trip takes four months, they aim the rockets to travel to the spot where Mars will be in four months.

This is an artist's drawing of what robot explorers to Mars might look like.

Martian robots

Several robots have already landed on Mars. Two *Viking* robots landed on Mars in 1976. These robots studied the soil to find out what it is made of. They set up weather stations to take temperatures and measure wind speed. In 1997, the *Mars Pathfinder* spacecraft landed on Mars. A tiny robot car called *Sojourner* was inside the spacecraft. Scientists on the Earth steered the car as it rolled around the surface. They used *Sojourner* to study what makes up the rocks on Mars.

Robots on Mars

Robots will be the first colonists to arrive on Mars. Sending robots to start a colony saves money and might save human lives. People would not have much time to start building their homes after their long trip. Their food, water and air supplies might run out before their new homes were ready.

Robot spacecraft would have equipment to prepare a colony for humans. They could use machines to suck in the Martian air, and separate the oxygen from the carbon dioxide gas. Then machines could make fuel from the carbon dioxide. Other robots could find ice, dig it up and melt it. The water could be stored in tanks.

A robot greenhouse could start food plants growing. The food would be ready to eat when humans arrive.

This is what future homes on Mars might look like.

People on Mars

After the robots have done their work, people could come to Mars. Scientists believe the first missions to Mars would be for short periods of time. Teams of astronauts would stay for one to two years and then return to the Earth.

The first human team on Mars would have lots of jobs to do. It would need to build homes, grow food and set up a power station.

The astronauts' first home would be their spacecraft. Then they could make temporary homes. Scientists believe astronauts will make homes out of airtight cloth tubes. Astronauts could unroll the tubes and pump oxygen inside them. Large straps on the tubes would anchor them to the ground. The straps would stop the homes blowing away. Inside the homes would be plastic tables, chairs and airbeds.

After a while, astronauts could set up more tubes. One tube could be a large greenhouse. Astronauts could grow more food to replace the food they eat from the robot greenhouse.

The first team would also need to set up a power station. The station would use solar panels to make electricity. They would also need an extra power station for emergencies. This power station would use special materials that heat up. The heat could be turned into electricity.

Astronauts would explore the planet after they build their homes. They would spend a lot of time collecting rocks to study and to use for building materials. The astronauts would also look for living things. There might be tiny living things hiding in the rocks or ice. There may also be fossils. Fossils are the remains of animals or plants that have turned to stone.

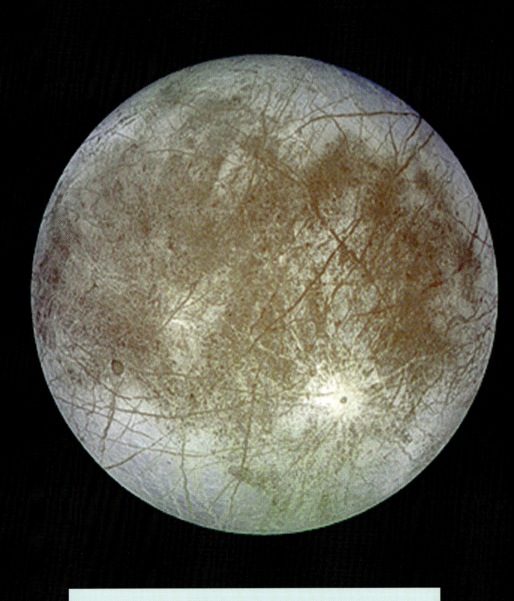

▲ Scientists think humans might be able to start a future colony on Europa.

The first team on Mars might stay for about a year. They could use the fuel the robots make to refuel their rocket. Then they could rocket back to the Earth.

A new team could then journey to Mars. The second team could live in the Martian homes built by the first team. They could set up new experiments and replace tools with newer ones. Some of the new tools could help them build permanent homes on Mars. The Mars rock could be used for building materials.

After many years, the first Martian base would be very large. More people could come to stay. They could build a glass dome over their homes to hold air.

Electric cars could carry people outside the dome. They could travel to places where robots **mine** rock and ice. They could explore Martian canyons.

Inside the dome, people could try to live normal lives. They could marry and have children. The children would become the first real Martians.

In time, people will build faster, more powerful rockets. They might use these rockets to take them to new places, such as Jupiter's moon Europa. There, they could create new homes and start building new space cities.

Glossary

atmosphere layer of gases that surrounds a planet

carbon dioxide gas made by burning carbon or when breathing out

gravity force that attracts all objects to each other; the gravitational force exerted by an object depends on its mass

meteorite (MEE-tee-or-rite) space rock that crashes into the surface of another object in space

mine to dig up valuable minerals and other resources that are underground

module tube-like section of a space station

orbit path an object travels around another object in space

resource something valuable or useful

satellite (SA-tuh-lite) object that orbits a larger object

Soviet Union country that is today known as the Russian Federation

Further information

Websites

BBC Science

http://www.bbc.co.uk/science/space/

British National Space Centre

http://www.bnsc.gov.uk/

European Space Agency

http://sci.esa.int/

**Star Child: A Learning Centre for
    Young Astronomers**

http://starchild.gsfc.nasa.gov/

Books

Our Universe: Moons, Gregory Vogt
    (Raintree Publishers, 2003)

Take Off!: Space Travel, Jenny Tesar
    (Heinemann Library, 2000)

Useful addresses

London Planetarium   The Science Museum

Marylebone Road   Exhibition Road

London NW1 5LR   London SW7 2DD

Index